# Early Settler Storybook

## Bobbie Kalman

**The Early Settler Life Series**

Crabtree Publishing Company

To Andrea, with love. May you never lose your
friendly smile, sunny disposition, and sense of
humor, which have added so many happy times
to our lives.

A very special thanks to the following people
who have made this book possible:

My excellent editorial and art staff: *Lise Gunby,
Nancy Cook, and Rosemary McLernon;*

The photographers who are responsible for the
faithful reproductions of old etchings, photographs,
and printed materials: *Sarah Peters and Stephen
Mangione;*

The historians and librarians who supplied us with
research and photographic opportunities: *William
Loos, Margaret Crawford Maloney, Dana Tenny,
and Jill Shefrin.*

*Cataloging in Publication Data*

*Kalman, Bobbie, 1947 –
    Early Settler Storybook*

*(Early settler life series)
Includes index.
ISBN 0-86505-021-X hardcover
ISBN 0-86505-020-1 softcover*

*1. Frontier and pioneer life   Juvenile fiction
2. Frontier and pioneer life   Juvenile poetry
I. Title.  II. Series*

*PZ7.K33Ea     JC818'.5409*

*102 Torbrick Avenue
Toronto M4J 4Z5*

*350 Fifth Avenue
Suite 3308
New York, N.Y. 10001*

# Contents

"She was hardly halfway across the river when the ice all around her gave way."

# Through settler's eyes

The stories and poems in this book show life as it was seen through the eyes of the settlers. The stories were written or took place more than one hundred years ago. They were written for settlers to read. Many of them are about settlers. Some words in the stories have been changed to make them easier to read today. The ideas and events in the stories have not been changed.

You will find that many of the stories and poems are about serious subjects. The writers of the nineteenth century did not usually write to entertain. They wrote to teach people values and virtues. In almost every story there is a lesson to be learned or a moral to be found. Good deeds were praised and bad acts were condemned.

# Stranded on ice

In the middle of the St. Lawrence River there is an island called St. Helen. Between the island and the shore the river runs swiftly, except in winter when the weather is so cold that the water freezes. Then in the spring, the melting snow creates a rush of water which rapidly breaks up the frozen surface. The icy blocks, tumbling, cracking, crumbling, roar onward to the sea.

There is always danger in crossing just before this takes place. One can not know the exact time at which the breakup will take place.

A small company of soldiers was stationed on the island of St. Helen. Many of the soldiers were repairing the road across it. Suddenly a thunderous crack announced that the breakup of the ice had begun. The ice heaved up, burst into pieces, and the whole mass gradually moved downwards, except a small part which remained attached to the shore of St. Helen.

## Up the river

Just at this moment a little girl was seen on the ice in the middle of the river. Without anyone's notice, she had attempted to cross the river alone. She was hardly halfway when the ice all around her gave way. The child's situation seemed hopeless.

Seeing her there, a young sergeant decided to go to her aid. Fixing his eyes on the child, he steadily struggled towards her. Sometimes just before him, sometimes just behind, a huge piece of ice would pause, rear up on end, and roll over, now and again hiding him from her view. Sometimes he was seen jumping from a piece that was beginning to rise, and then, like a white bear, carefully clambering down a piece that was beginning to sink. On he went until he reached the little island of ice on which the child stood. The soldier held her firmly in his arms and began to think about how they could reach safety.

## Out of sight

Both the soldier and the child had floated so far down the river that their movements were no longer visible to the naked eye. The soldier's comrades watched them through spy-glasses as the sergeant either led the child or carried her. He continued in this way until he was entirely out of the sight of his comrades. They gave them both up as lost.

The two continued on from ice floe to ice floe until they were discovered towards evening by some sailors. At great risk, these sailors pushed off in a boat and rescued the two. Both were taken to the home of one of the sailors. A few days later the girl was happily reunited with her parents. The brave sergeant quietly returned to his barracks.

Grace and her father struggle hard against the waves. They must save the men on the sinking ship!

# The daring Darlings

It was on the morning of September 7, 1838, at daybreak, that John Darling, the lighthouse keeper of the Longstone lighthouse, saw a steamer in the distance being dashed to pieces on the rocks by the fury of the waves.

Several of the crew of the ill-fated ship were clinging to the wreck. They expected every wave to sweep them into the boiling sea. What was to be done? Could any help be given? Would the poor sailors be saved from a watery grave?

Although the storm was raging frightfully, Grace Darling and her father decided to rescue their fellow human beings. They knew that they would be risking their lives. They launched their small boat through the stormy sea and rowed towards the wrecked ship. Now on the crest of the wave, then in the deep valley of the sea, the father and daughter strained to reach the wreck in time to save the sailors. At last they were at the sinking ship. They struggled to pull the nine poor sailors into their boat. So furious was the storm, that it took Grace and her father three hours to row the shipwrecked sailors back to the lighthouse.

Grace Darling's name was spoken of in all parts of the country. She became an instant heroine. Her fame even reached Europe. It is said that many offers of marriage were made to her, but she preferred to remain the companion and assistant of her father.

This little story suggests to us that no matter in what situation we are placed, whether in the busy scenes of life, or in a lonely place, we have it in our power to show love, charity, and courage to those who need our help.

# The last quarrel

One day, a Newfoundland dog and a mastiff had a big quarrel over a bone. They were fighting on a bridge, and over they went into the water. The banks were so high, that they were forced to swim some distance before they came to a landing place. It was very easy for the Newfoundland; he was as much at home in the water as a seal. But not so poor Bruce: he struggled and tried his best to swim, but made little headway. The Newfoundland dog quickly reached the land, and then turned to look at his old enemy. He saw plainly that Bruce's strength was fast failing, and that he was likely to drown. So what did the noble fellow do but plunge in, seize him gently by the collar, and, keeping his nose above water, tow him safely into port! It was funny to see these dogs look at each other as they shook their coats. Their glance said as plainly as words, "We'll never quarrel any more."

*A sign of true friendship is risking one's life for another.*

*"Quick! Let's run for it!" Mabel shouted. "Back towards the house!"*

# Caught in a ring of fire

"Children, I will dismiss you now. The air is becoming so thick with smoke that I'm afraid bush fires have broken out not far away. All of you had better get home as soon as possible."

Miss Ada Nelson, teacher of a country school, said this at about three o'clock on the afternoon of Monday, October 9, 1871. In less than two minutes the log schoolhouse was empty.

For six weeks there had been little or no rain. Disastrous fires were breaking out daily, consuming the dried up grass of open fields as well as the dead trees and underbrush of forests.

When the school children separated in different directions, one little party took a road leading directly north. This group was made up of Mabel Howard, a well-grown girl of sixteen, and the top scholar in the school; Gus Boylan, a tall boy of seventeen who walked with her; and Tim and Harry Lennox, aged eleven and nine years. The parents of these children lived on adjoining farms three miles from the schoolhouse, in a neighborhood not likely to be reached by bush fires. The young people had no fears for the safety of their own homes. All went well with them until they came to a belt of pine where they saw many dry treetops, left on the ground by the log cutters the winter before.

## "We must save the children!"

The party had not gone more than a few steps when they found the heat unbearable. "Back, back to the clearing! We can't get through!" cried Mabel. The quartet retreated rapidly. They stood a moment, bewildered, and then Mabel exclaimed suddenly in a horrified tone, "Oh, those poor children, Richard, Gertrude, and Crissy Moore! I met their mother this morning on her way to the general store. She told me that Mr. Moore had gone east with a drove of cattle. She had left the children alone in the house. The fire will

be sure to fly over that narrow field and catch the house and barn. Unless we can save them, the poor things will be burned to death. Come, boys, come! We can out-run the fire and get there in time to take those babies out of danger."

"I don't risk my life to save anybody's brats. Let them take their chances," replied Gus Boylan.

Mabel Howard glared at him and cried, "Oh, you cruel person! Be a coward if you must. I can't leave those children to die."

## Risking her life

Tim and Harry Lennox dumbly followed Gus. Mabel was left alone to carry out a rescue which might very well cost her her own life.

She ran over the field towards the house. She could feel the heat of the flames closing in behind her. She hoped she could run faster than the flames could spread. She reached the house. She threw open the door and called for the children. No answer.

"Where could they be? There is such little time!"

Suddenly she heard little voices wailing in the direction of the forest. She ran towards the sound and found the children on the ground crying their little hearts out. There was no place for them to run. The fire was closing in on all sides.

"Quick! Let's run for it!" Mabel shouted. "Back towards the house!" They ran as fast as their tiny feet could carry them. Mabel grabbed Richard and carried him.

When they reached the house, Mabel realized that the fire was coming across the field. It was racing towards them. There was no way to turn. Smoke was blowing at them in thick columns. Only a miracle could save them now!

*"Stay still down there, Richard! Crissy is coming down next."*

## Saved by the well

Mabel grew frightened. She could not think. Suddenly, as if her eyes were directed by a mysterious force, she saw the well.

"The well!" she shouted. "We must lower ourselves down into the well. There will be enough air in there for us for at least a few hours. Smoke rises. The well is below ground. The smoke will not reach us, nor will the flames."

Mabel lowered the children down one by one in the bucket. The water in the well was shallow enough that the children were not in danger of drowning. When all three children were in, Mabel slid down the rope after them. There they waited to be rescued. They did not mind the cold water at all. After the scorching heat of the fire, they were just comfortable. Mabel kept the children from being afraid by telling them funny stories. They sang songs to pass the time. It did not take long for the fire to burn everything in sight.

A few hours later a woman staggered through the fields to the south. Her grief was so great she could hardly make her way to what used to be her home. She stood one moment in stupefied horror. Then she threw up her hands in an agony of despair and wildly shrieked, "Gone, gone! My darlings have perished!"

But what was that? Her heart-breaking cry was answered by a muffled shout. She forced herself to be absolutely quiet. The shout seemed to come from the bowels of the earth. She followed the sounds which led her to the well. Then she heard a familiar voice, "It is I, Mabel Howard, Mrs. Moore. Richard, Gertrude, and Crissy are alive and well."

## The joyful reunion

Mrs. Moore was beside herself with joy. She pulled her children up on the rope. They all hugged and kissed each other, so happy to be together again. Mabel climbed up the rope last. Mrs. Moore cried tears of joy and could not stop hugging Mabel. She was so grateful to this wonderful brave girl.

It wasn't long before Mr. Moore arrived on the happy scene. He had managed to sell his cattle at a high price. They would be able to build another home right away. The Moores soon replaced the lost house and barn. Mabel Howard was the guest of honor at the housewarming party.

*Throw a blanket quickly around him!*

# Fire!

Alas! what a sight for a mother to see!
Devouring flames encircle her child.
In vain the poor fellow endeavors to flee
With cries, so heart-rending and wild.

He rushes along in his bitter despair,
Attempting escape from the fire,

But only increases the current of air
That fans the flame higher and higher.

Alas! must he perish? Can nothing be done?
Poor mother! oh, might you not throw
A blanket around that poor suffering one,
And stifle the terrible foe?

*"I've had no kind words till now."*

# Life without parents

*Many children were without homes in the eighteenth and nineteenth centuries. Today the government helps to look after homeless children. They are cared for in orphanages or by foster parents. In the old days, there were few, if any, orphanages. Children roamed the cities or countryside hoping to make enough money to feed themselves. The story below is about a girl who was more fortunate than most orphaned or abandoned children. A wealthy man had just opened an orphanage in the town nearby.*

# The wildflower orphan

"Buy some flowers from a poor orphan," said a soft, sad voice. The man with the top hat and gold walking stick turned. The girl was only about ten years old. She peered up at the man from behind a tangle of copper curls. Her dress was clean and her face had been scrubbed until it was pink, but already a smudge of yellow pollen colored her nose. She held a bouquet of flowers that she must have picked on the roadside leading into town. The flowers were as wild and as pretty as she.

The man could not help smiling. Many poor girls were forced to sell flowers for a living, but most managed to find fancy roses. She held out a trembling hand in the shape of a cup. The man reached into his pocket and pulled out a few coins. He held them above her cupped hand.

"And where does this poor orphan live?" he asked. "My father is dead and my mother gone off with a new husband," she replied. The tears began to trickle down her cheeks. "I've had no kind words till now," she sniffled.

The man put the coins back in his pocket. The wildflower girl hung her head.

"Promise to be good and I shall find you a home," the man said. "Yes, sir, yes sir," the girl said eagerly.

## A home at last

The man with the top hat and the gold cane took the girl by the hand. She went with him, clutching her wildflowers. He led her to the home for orphans which had just opened in the next town.

The little girl learned later that the man who had saved her also had donated the money that supported the orphans' home.

He often came to visit the orphan children with his son. One day many years later, the wildflower girl and the son were married.

## Happily ever after

Their wedding was a happy occasion at the orphanage. All the children were invited to attend. Some of the smaller girls, dressed in beautiful new dresses, walked behind the bride carrying bouquets of wildflowers.

The wildflower girl and her husband adopted three children from the orphans' home. They continued to visit the other orphan children regularly. Every time they visited they brought with them a big bouquet of fresh wildflowers. The flowers gave the other orphans hope that they too would someday have happy homes of their own.

*All the orphans attended the wedding of the wildflower girl. She adopted three of the children soon after.*

# Hannah waits by the spring alone

Low on the meadows the shadows lie,
The sun shines bright in the eastern
sky,

And the merry robin begins his lay
To greet the joy of the coming day;

The gentle breath of the summer breeze
Its secret tells to the whispering trees,

And the swelling ears of the tasseled
corn
Grow full in the breath of the August
morn.

The world in wonderful beauty lies
'Neath the glowing smile of the sunny
skies,

When Hannah her bucket hastens to
bring
Where the water drips from the crystal
spring.

Her heart is weary, her step is slow,
As she sadly watches its cooling flow.

Once more has the dreary round begun
That is ushered in by each day's sun;

For a weary life has Hannah had
And her patient face has grown so sad

Till the radiant joy of a day new born
No echo finds in her heart forlorn.

Against the rock does she sadly lean,
With a drooping head and a helpless
mien,

And often the bitter teardrops rise
In the gloomy depths of the soft dark
eyes

As she sadly pauses upon the stone
To think of the days when, not alone,

To the flowing spring she would wander
down
To fill the bucket so cracked and brown,

And then to the old house on the farm
It was carried back by a stronger arm.

But down by the hill where the streamlet
flows,
There, sad and solemn, a yew tree grows,

And a stately column of marble tall,
Stands pure and white where the shadows
fall.

A quiet sleeper lies 'neath the stone,
And Hannah waits by the spring alone.

*Hannah remembers Father.*

14

*"How sad we are now we're alone, I wish my mother were not dead!"*

# Missing Mother

Leaving her play, in thoughtful tone
A young girl to her father said,
'How sad we are now we're alone, -
I wish my mother were not dead!'

'I can remember she was fair,
And how she kindly looked and smiled,
When she would fondly stroke my hair,
And call me her beloved child.'

'Before my mother went away,
You never sighed as you do now,
You used to join us in our play,
And be our merriest playmate too.'

'Poor little Ted and I that day,
We sat within our silent room,

But we could neither read nor play,
The very walls seemed full of gloom.'

'I wish my mother had not died,
We never have been glad since then,
They say, and is it true,' she cried,
'That she can never come again?'

The father checked his tears, and thus
He spake, 'My child they do not err
Who say she cannot come to us,
But you and I may go to her.'

'Remember your dear mother still,
And the good lessons she has given;
Like her be humble, free from ill,
And you shall see her face in heaven.'

# Amanda and Jeremy search for a home

*"What shall become of us?" cried Amanda.*

Amanda and Jeremy had lost both of their parents. Their father died of diphtheria on the ocean voyage from England. Their mother fell ill shortly after they arrived at the homestead. She died soon afterwards. The two children were all alone in the world.

"What shall become of us?" cried Amanda. "We will not go back! We will find a new home," insisted Jeremy. "There must be some folks nearby who could use two children to help with the chores."

The two young orphans walked for days through the forest. They followed the setting sun. They knew there was a town somewhere west of their homestead. They had brought with them all the food they could carry from home, but they had eaten the last of it at noon.

That night it was Jeremy who cried himself to sleep. He missed the warmth of his mother's arms as she had always hugged him before he went to bed. This time Amanda reassured him.

"Mother is in heaven. But she can still see everything we do. She will help us to find a new home where people will love us."

## The best mother in the world

Jeremy was not so certain. He had always felt he had the best mother in the world. She did not scold the way other mothers did. His friend, Tommy Miller, was always getting the stick when he came back all dirty from playing. Jeremy's mother understood how children sometimes got into mischief. Jeremy was sure there was no one on earth as kind as his mother had been. He fell asleep dreaming of her that night.

The children awoke early the next morning and by eight o'clock they had reached the nearest town. Amanda thought they should go to the general store and tell the storekeeper their problem. Storekeepers always knew everyone in the area. Perhaps this one would have an idea of where they could go.

## Caleb Silk's idea

The storekeeper's name was Caleb Silk. He welcomed the children and told them to warm up by the stove. He went upstairs to get his wife. Mrs. Silk brought down fresh bread, cheese, and a glass of milk for each of them. They ate hungrily as they told their sad story.

"You're not the first orphans to come through these parts," said the storekeeper. "It seems that this country is rougher than some folks can bear. Why, we've had at least three like you in the last month. We had better find a place for you to stay before the snow comes. For then no children can survive the outdoors for long. You can stay here for a few nights. If no one takes you in before Sunday, well, the next town is just another day's walk."

That night Amanda and Jeremy slept peacefully above the general store. While the children slept, Caleb Silk took a ride out to the Stewart's farm. Abe and Betty

Stewart had been kind enough to take in the last three orphans who had passed through Caleb's store. They had a lot of land and needed the extra hands for farming.

The Stewarts had two children of their own. Two months before they had taken in the three orphans. They told Caleb that they had no room, but that they would at least come to the store to meet the children the next day.

## Room for two more

When Betty Stewart first looked at the two children, she could not believe her eyes. Amanda was the spitting image of herself at that age! And Jeremy seemed like such a fine boy. Yet where would they find room to put two more children? Perhaps Jeremy could share the loft with two of the orphan boys and Amanda could sleep on a trundle bed in the girls' room. Betty knew the other children were crowded in the two rooms. But her heart had gone out to the newcomers. Abe and Betty decided they could give Amanda and Jeremy a home.

That night the two children met Melissa, Mary, Judith, Rodney, and Michael. A great deal of grumbling took place when the children learned that there would be another person sharing their rooms. Why, they were crowded to the limit already!

The girls took Amanda in without too much coaxing. With Jeremy, however, it was a different story. Rodney and Michael made fun of him when he cried that night. Not only had he lost his mother, but now Amanda was no longer at his side. The boys teased him and called him a "crybaby." That made him even more upset. Surely he would never be happy in this home!

In the next few weeks Amanda adjusted completely to her new family. There was a lot of work to do, but Abe and Betty were very kind. Betty fussed over her as if Amanda were her natural child. However, Jeremy was not quite as happy. He had been the apple of his mother's eye and Betty seemed hardly to notice him. It was clear to him that she would never love him. He still longed for his mother and cried for her every night.

Jeremy made up his mind to search for his mother. He would run away in the night when nobody was looking. Amanda had once told him that heaven was in a high place. He was sure that if he climbed the highest hill he could find, he would be able to see his mother.

## Jeremy runs away

The next day, as the other children went about their chores, Jeremy started on his way. About noon it started to snow. It was coming down so fast that he could hardly see anything in front of him. Shivering with cold, he huddled near a tree and decided to wait out the storm.

When Amanda discovered Jeremy was gone she grew frightened. She knew that he would head for the nearby hill. He had often told her that he would climb it to be closer to his mother in heaven.

*Shivering with cold, he huddled near a tree and decided to wait out the storm.*

Amanda stared down over the cliff, sure that Jeremy had fallen off the precipice.

18

# Braving the blizzard

Amanda slipped away from the house without telling anyone. She made her way to the hill through the blinding snow. She just had to find Jeremy before he froze to death! Her strong determination to bring her brother back kept her from succumbing to the cold. Amanda climbed for two hours. The wind was blowing hard. She kept sliding backwards. But she just had to get to the top!

When Abe and Betty stopped work for lunch, they noticed the children were gone. Alarmed, Abe, Michael, Rodney, and some of the neighbors formed a search party to locate the missing children. They found Jeremy soon enough. He was still huddled by the tree. His fingers and toes were nearly frozen. Abe asked him where he had planned to go. Reluctantly, Jeremy revealed why he was heading for the mountain.

Rodney and Michael took him back to the house. Abe and the other men started their difficult trek to the mountain. The blizzard blinded the men completely. To keep track of each other they tied themselves together with a long rope. They shouted out Amanda's name over and over. There was no reply. Abe led them to a ridge halfway up the mountain. It was a dangerous climb, but he had to take the chance that Amanda would be there. If not, they would be forced by the deep snow and lack of visibility to give up their search.

There she was! She was staring down over the cliff, sure that Jeremy had fallen off the precipice. She was in shock and could not even hear their cries. Abe picked her up. He reassured her that Jeremy was safe and warm back at the house. The neighbors formed a line again and made their way through the blizzard back to home.

## Jeremy learns about love

When everyone was safe at last, they all wept for joy by the fire. Betty held Jeremy in her lap. She comforted him as he blamed himself for putting everyone in so much danger. The other children were happy to see their new brother and sister safe. And Jeremy, in Betty's arms, felt that he had found a new mother at last.

*Abe reassured Amanda that Jeremy was safe.*

19

# The great outdoors

*In the merry month of June, life is all a holiday.*

The settlers loved the outdoors. In spring they looked forward to the blooming flowers. In summer they romped in the meadows and frolicked in the lakes and streams. The fall was harvest time. There were crops to be brought in. Both children and adults enjoyed the outdoor work. It was followed by corn roasts, big suppers, dancing, and games.

The settlers especially loved winter sports and activities. They traveled to visit friends, neighbors, and relatives. They went skating, sledding, and tobogganing. The more adventurous types wandered for hours in the woods on snowshoes.

In those days people were able to enjoy the outdoors because it surrounded them. Their senses were tuned in to the sights and sounds of nature. Today most of us have to drive for hours before we find open spaces. Read the following outdoor poems and try to imagine what the settlers saw and felt in a world ruled by Mother Nature.

## In the merry month of June

It is the merry month of June,
The flowers are fresh and fair,
The birds are warbling among the boughs,
No sorrow anywhere.

The streams are singing as they leap
So merrily along,
The trees are bending on the brink,
And listening to the song.

The apple orchard's all in bloom,
The bee is humming by,
There's gladness in the gay green earth,
And rapture in the sky.

The schoolboys in the leafy woods,
Are busy at their play,
And merrily they shout, for life
Is all a holiday.

*Little Meg was resting, tired out from play.*

# A bright summer day

All among the daisies,
On a summer day,
Little Meg was resting,
Tired out with play,
Underneath the oak tree,
Where the ivy clings,
And the blackbird to his mate
A merry carol sings;
Butterflies flit by her,
Wild bees hum around,
And the rippling river
Makes a pleasant sound.
Music in the water,
Music in the air,
Music in the bird's note,
Music everywhere.
Little Meg sat listening.
Suddenly said she,
"Mother, there are voices
Speaking unto me."
"Tell me," said her mother,
"What the voices say."

Little Meg said softly,
"Everything today
Says I am so happy!
For the sun shines bright,
And the flowers are beautiful,
And earth is full of light."

*Little Meg smelled each flower that she picked. The world was filled with beautiful sights, smells, and sounds.*

21

*The settlers loved riding in their sleighs.   They bundled up warm under heavy fur blankets.*

# Sleighbells in the snow

O'er the smooth and glittering snow,
Merrily, merrily off we go –
Nature sleeps, and not a sound
Breaks the stillness all around,
While the horses' feet keep time
To the sleigh bells' tuneful chime.

Now we pass the village street,
Where the varying pathways meet;
Now across the fields we fly,
Where the wildflowers buried lie;
Buried, in their shroud of snow,
Till the summer breezes blow.

Now we gain the frozen stream,
Where the icy atoms gleam;
Say, could they have brighter been
Were they gems to deck a queen?
Who would think that down below
Still the rapid waters flow?

Now we take the homeward way,
Warned by the departing day;
From the windows, o'er the snow,
See the bright fires' ruddy glow;
Their mute welcome seems akin
To the faces bright within.

*A heavy snowfall usually meant plenty of work clearing the road to the farmhouse. The poor horse pulls as the boys hitch a free ride on the homemade snowplow.*

# Snow, beautiful snow

Snow, snow everywhere!
On the ground and in the air,
In the fields and in the lane,
On the roof and window pane.

Snow, snow everywhere!
Making common things look fair -
Stones beside the garden walks,
Broken sticks and cabbage stalks.

Snow, snow everywhere!
Dressing up the trees so bare,
Resting on each fir-tree bough,
Till it bends, a plume of snow.

Snow, snow everywhere!
Covering up young roots with care,
Keeping them so safe and warm,
Jack Frost cannot do them harm.

Snow, snow everywhere!
We are glad to see it here;
Snowball-making will be fun
When tomorrow's work is done!

*Tobogganing, sledding, and snowballing were favorite snow activities.*

23

*"We're ready for the attack. Let's give it to them, boys!"*

# Snowballing

The snow, the snow, the fairy snow, the pure white falling snow!
How pulses leap and hearts beat high, and cheeks with color glow,

To throw the soft white balls about, with shouts of happy glee;
And mirth and mischief, hand in hand, show friendly rivalry.

24

*"On the other hand, let's wave the white flag of peace and retreat."*

The snow, the snow, the glorious snow,
in thick flakes showering down,
The city roofs, the country trees, with
fair white wreaths to crown;

As falls from heaven the feathery shower
upon the earth below,
How many youthful tongues exclaim, "Oh,
welcome back the snow!"

THE NORTH WIND DOTH BLOW.

To JOSIE NEMBACH.

S. B. MILLS.

The north wind doth blow, And we shall have snow, And what will poor Rob-in do then, poor thing? He'll sit in a barn, And to keep him-self warm Will hide his head un-der his wing, poor thing!

The north wind doth blow,
And we shall have snow
And what will the Robin do then,
poor thing?

He'll sit in a barn,
And to keep himself warm
Will hide his head under his wing,
poor thing!

# In February

The wind it blew, the rain it fell,
   a little maid I met.
"Alas, my pretty one!" I said,
   "you're getting very wet!
What name 'befits so fair a face?"
   She answered

Your eyes are quite as blue" I said,
   "as any flower that blows.
The ruffian Wind has dared to kiss
   your cheek until it glows."
And softly in her downcast face
   The lovely color

While I am standing here Sweetheart, the rain is quite forgot,
O will you let me walk with you from this enchanted spot.
   And be my little Valentine?"
      She said "I'd rather

"Nay, Dear," I pleaded tenderly "Prithee, be not so coy
I am your servant, suppliant, slave, — your smile my only joy.
   "O please to go away!" she said,
      You're nothing but a

Now when she spoke so cruelly, and turned a scornful shoulder,
The day seemed darker than before, the very wind blew colder,
   But plucking courage from despair
      I felt my heart grow

"Alas, I see it all!" I said, "I am indeed undone!
There is some other happier swain who has your favor won
   She dropped her eyes upon the ground
      And faintly murmured

"Nay then," I cried, "my heart is yours, — be yours
   this shelter too!"
She put her finger in her mouth "I'm getting just
   wet through
   I think" she murmured, very low,
      "I'd better go with

In the poem above there are seven words that are not given. You have to
guess these from the picture clues at the ends of the stanzas. We will give
you the words upside-down and in the wrong order. Try to guess the missing
words without looking at the upside-down list.

Words:   not, none, boy, you, violet, bolder

27

*Animals were a big part of settler life. Most of the settlers were farmers. They depended on animals for food, clothing, transportation and companionship. It is not surprising that many of the stories and poems read by the settlers were about animals. Most of these animal stories were really about human characteristics. The story below is full of animal expressions. Can you find all of them? How many are there? What does each one mean? Why do people use these expressions? Which animal expressions do you often use?*

# Human nature seen through animal stories

The teacher, who was as clever as a monkey, told his students to stop their monkey-business. "Be as quick as bunnies and form a snake in front of me. Bobby Bear, you are moving at a snail's pace. Follow Peter Pig like a lemming and stop badgering Freddy Fox, you bird-brain!

"Samuel, you are letting the cat out of the bag to Darryl Dog. You can stop your cattiness right now, or your goose will be cooked. Darryl, you don't have to be Samuel's faithful dog. You will lead a dog's life if you continue to follow him like a sheep.

"Freddy Fox, don't be so sly. It gets my goat that you think you can cheat on your exams. I got it straight from the horse's mouth. And you, Bobby Bear!

Just take a gander at yourself. You are as dirty as a pig. I can't bear to look at you.

"And as for you, Ronald Rabbit, you too are acting fishy. You will never be as wise as an owl if you continue to hound Peter Pig. Just because he is as playful as a kitten does not mean you can bully him forever.

"Yes, as far as I can see, you are nothing but a bunch of turkeys! Just because you are quiet as mice right now does not mean you can weasel anything out of me! There is only one of you who will be as happy as a lark in the future. Billy, who is always as busy as a beaver, will have the lion's share of success."

*The horse flung the cruel boy over the fence. Was there a lesson to be learned from this story?*

*The goat watched the boy fall on the ground with a thud. "Just look at the shape you're in," mused the goat.*

# It really got his goat!

A horse and goat were in the habit of grazing together in a field. A gang of young rascals got into the field, and amused themselves by chasing the goat and throwing stones at it. This they did on several occasions, and each time that the horse saw its friend attacked, it galloped up to the rescue, and drove the boys off. One day one of them struck the goat with a stick. The horse immediately seized the boy by the collar of his jacket and flung him clear over the palings into the road. The goat watched as if to say, "Sticks and stones may hurt my skin, but just look at the shape you're in!"

## The medicine cat

*Emily Harris lived all alone. She was very ill with scarlet fever. She was so weak that she could hardly keep her eyes open. The doctor told Emily to take her medicine every four hours. However, Emily could not keep track of the time. She was delirious with fever. Her cat, Cecil, acted as her doctor. He woke her up every few hours to make sure she took her medicine. Emily would not have survived without the loving care of her loyal cat.*

*Pussy tries her paw at playing the fiddle. She must have heard about "Hey diddle, diddle."*

## Cat and the fiddle

Hey! diddle, diddle,
The cat and the fiddle,
The cow jumped over the moon;
The little dog laughed
To see the sport,
While the dish ran after the spoon.

*Since these two pets are "the cat's meow," they find "no use in crying over spilt milk." What do these two expressions mean?*

# A terrible scratch

Oh, pussy! you naughty, ungrateful old cat,
To scratch me because I just gave you a pat
When you would not draw dolly across the floor.
I had harnessed you tight with a scarlet cord,
And had promised to give you some cream as reward,
And a couple of sardines; what could I do more?
Now dolly's as light as a feather, you know,
And the carriage almost of itself will go;
Yet you would not pull at it, but tried to get loose,
And entangled yourself, and the carriage upset,
And then the wheel broke, and you got in a fret;
And for your behavior there was no excuse.
Just look how my finger is bleeding. Oh dear!
How it hurts me; it will not get well soon, I fear!
Now are you not sorry I am in such pain?
No sardines or cream you shall have, puss, from me;
And a very long time you will find it will be
Before I play horses with you, puss, again.

*"It will be a long time, puss, before I play with you again!"*

*"You would not pull my dolly, yet you give kitty a ride."*

31

*Thirteen little pigs run away from home to try the world out on their own. They discover the hard way that freedom is sometimes not what it seems to be. Read the poem about the pigs' adventures. What is the author's message to children who read this poem? Give all the reasons why you think running away might be dangerous for children.*

# The thirteen little pigs

Do you know old Philip Spudbury, that
works at Pixham Mill?
He has thirteen little baby pigs that are
hardly ever still;
'Twould make you laugh to see them; do
just peep into their sty!
They're still just for a moment, and with
all their heads awry,
Each gives you such a saucy look from
a twinkling little eye.
Then scamper, scamper, scamper, all
around the sty they run,
And jump and dive, and tumble, they
so enjoy the fun.

Except their curly little tails, they are
all as white as snow,
But their little curly tails are as black
as black can go.
And Philip likes to see them clean, so
washes them each night, -
In fact, these thirteen little pigs are
Philip's great delight;
And to see them in the washing-tub is
such a funny sight -
There was never such a splash-a-dash,
such a sputter, such a splutter,
As when these little pigs go in what
Philip calls the *wutter*.

There is a wash they all enjoy, 'tis not
a wash outside,
But a kind of wash they take within their
oily little hides:
A mess of pig-potatoes, mixed up with
barley meal:
Such a grunting, such a groaning, such
an overflow of zeal:
Such lengths of quiet gobbling, such
intervals of squeal,
You never heard before or since; for
I'll undertake to say
That children who read this take their
meals in a mannerly way.

Now Philip always when his work at
Pixham Mill is done,
Would take these thirteen little pigs for
a pleasant little run
Along the grassy roadside; they'd all kick
up their heels
And tumble out their laughter in merry
little squeals.

Poke their noses through the hedges, and
sniff at turnip fields,
But never would their master let one
little piggie stray
From off the smooth and grassy slope to
the neighboring dusty way.

One luckless day the miller had a very
heavy grind,
And honest Philip Spudbury was obliged
to stay behind;
Now this the pigs resented and declared
it all a shame,
Held an 'Indignation Meeting,' at which
all thirteen came
To an angry verdict that the miller
was to blame.
To see them stamp, and rave, and rant,
and shake their grave heads after,
Would have made a serious person even
almost die of laughter.

## Running away from home

The garden gate stood open wide - there
was not a soul in sight;
So off they scampered up the road in
pure and great delight.
Oh! the glorious enjoyment of freedom
just acquired!
Oh! what will children and pigs not do
by liberty inspired!
And oh! the joy a *pig* can find in getting
all bemired!
They rolled about the dusty road, they
dabbled in the ditches,
Till their snow-white coats seemed wrapped
around with dirty coats and breeches.

Now up the road, about a mile, there was
a muddy pool,
Where croaking frogs, and crawling newts,
and tadpoles kept a school.
The mud was thick and slimy and black as
blackest ink;
Oh, what a squeal of shrill delight burst
out upon the brink,
When the thirteen little pigs came up! and
then to see them sink,
And roll and wallow in that mud! It would
have made poor Philip sad,
And I'm sure you all will think with me
their conduct very bad.

*The little pigs found their way into a neighbor's farmyard. They thought it was great fun to frighten these poor children. They grunted and squealed with their newly found sense of power.*

## Hopelessly lost

But night was coming quickly now and
suppertime drew nigh.
The pigs began to think of home and
started for the sty.
But alas! they missed the turning and
wandered far away,
And on and on and on they went, and
hearts that once were gay
Were filled with gloom and sadness now,
and no familiar ray
Of home appeared to gladden them, and
no one did they meet
To guide towards home those heavy hearts
and very heavy feet.

At last, when darkening evening was
closing into night,
They heard a heavy foostep and saw a
welcome light.
With joy they hurried towards it, and
soon there came in view
A sight which each one recognized, a
monster dressed in blue,

Which made each little foot to shake
within each little shoe.
'Twas the butcher! with a lantern, and
in his belt a knife.
Oh, how the piggies squealed and ran
as if for very life!

But as they ran from one mishap, another
came instead,
Of goats, and sheep, and cows, and pigs,
and cats and dogs the dread.
The butcher he was dressed in blue but
this was flaming red!
With yellow breeches on his legs, a cocked
hat on his head,
His waistcoat of the brightest green; with
fear they would have fled,
But alas! they were exhausted: so the
keeper, Mr. Buffer,
To the dreadful pound took off each one
a vagrant doom to suffer.

## Mistaken identities

The pound was formed by four high walls
and open to the sky;
No bed was there, no straw, nor any
comfort of the sty.
So, huddled in one corner, they tried to
go to sleep,
When they heard a voice that made each
heart with joy and gladness leap,
And through the gate they dimly saw
their kind old master peep.
'I told you, Mr. Spudbury,' they heard
the keeper say,
'These pigs are *black*, they can't be
yours, so please to go away!'

'Oh, so they are,' said Philip; 'where can
the rascals roam?
I must give them up for lost tonight and
hasten off back home,
For the clouds are dark and lowering; we
shall have a heavy rain.
And early in the morning I will search for
them again,
For searching more on this dark night
will be to search in vain.'
And the quick retreating footsteps told
the pigs all hope was over,
And they'd better sleep on the hard cold
ground as they could not sleep in clover.

In the morning just before 'twas light
they woke up in a shiver,
And found the rain was falling down upon
them like a river.
Ah, how they wished themselves all safe
and housed at home once more.
But then you know some time ago they
thought all that a bore,
But they'd been about the world a bit,
grown wiser than before.
The rainbow-colored evening cloud is
nought but mists and vapors,
And they found the world that looked so
bright not formed for cutting capers.

Now the mighty Mr. Buffer, before his
morning's meal
Went off to see his captives with all a
jailor's zeal:
When looking through the gate to see if
everything went right,
He stood, and stared, and stared again,
for all the pigs were white!
He left them black as ink, he thought, as
late as yesternight.
'Twas comical to witness his astonishing
surprise,
For he knew not that the friendly rain
had washed off their disguise.

## Sty-high!

Oh, joy! joy! joy! once more was heard
their master's gentle tone.
The gate was open wide as wide and all
their grief was gone!
They sniffed about his well-known boots,
they gamboled all around him,
They poked each other in the side for joy
that they had found him;
And as for Mr. Buffer, they felt inclined
to pound him.
But forgiving him, they walked off home
as fast as they could toddle,
And ate barley meal with such a zeal that
they could hardly waddle.

*Ah, to be babied once more! Philip
Spudbury gives the smallest pig water
from a bottle. Lionel the pig is happy
to be home.*

*Animals were thought to have certain characteristics. Hares were often shown in races with other animals. This story has no words. It is up to you to write them. Write a story, comic strip, poem, or joke about Rover's race. Will there be a moral to your story?*

# A bear for punishment

Settlers were always battling bears. Can you write a funny story using the pictures above and all the words in the following list: bear, bare, bearing, barrel, barreling, barrier, bear arms, bear up, bare-handed, bare-headed. Can you think of any more "bear" expressions?

# If!

If you saw a goat
Buttoned in a coat;
If you saw a rat
Dressed up in a hat;
If you saw a deer
Drink some ginger beer;
If you saw a lamb
Take a slice of ham;
If you saw a bear
Combing out its hair;
If you saw a seal
Riding on a wheel;
If you saw an ox
Opening a box;
If you saw a pig
Eat a nice new fig;
If you saw a mouse
Throwing down a house;
If you saw a stag
Picking up a rag;
If you saw a cow
Make a pretty bow;
If you saw a fly
Take its slate and cry –
You would surely say,
"What peculiar play!"
Or would surely sing,
"What a funny thing!"

# Wolf attacks

The settlers were always on the lookout for wolves. Travelers were scared to death of them. Settlers' diaries are filled with advice on how to get rid of wolves. There are many accounts of "menacing wolves." The "menace", however, always seemed to be just a howl in the distance. There was even one story in which a settler's son was *believed* to have been eaten by a pack of wolves. But to our knowledge, in the days of the settlers, there were no proven records of wolf attacks in North America.

For some reason the wolf has received unfair press coverage for hundreds of years. In stories, such as "The Three Little Pigs" and "Little Red Riding Hood," the wolf is definitely the villain. Perhaps the writers of those stories knew something we do not know.

We have found several wolf stories in old children's magazines. They all have the same plot. The wolf attacks, and the wolf is killed. The following story was said to be true. Read it, and then do some research on wolves. Conservation groups can give you good information. Then you decide whether or not the story could be true. Has the wolf's name been smeared by unfair publicity?

*A vicious wolf appeared out of nowhere.*

# The loyal pet

The Andersons lived in a log cabin on the edge of the forest. They were new settlers. There was no door on their log cabin because Mr. Anderson did not have the tools needed to make one. A blanket hung over the opening.

The Andersons had a new baby just two months old. Their dog, Sam, was devoted to the child. One day, Mr. Anderson was busy chopping trees in the forest. Mrs. Anderson went to fetch water from the nearby spring. The baby was alone in her crib. Suddenly, a wolf appeared out of nowhere and leapt on the bassinet. Sam, the dog, did not waste a second. He jumped on the wolf and bit its neck. The wolf, badly injured, staggered back to the forest. The baby did not even have a chance to cry, thanks to the quick action taken by the loyal pet.

*Before the baby had a chance to cry, Sam attacked the wolf and saved the day.*

*Does this cunning fox look as if he could be outwitted? Read "Outfoxed" and find out!*

# Outfoxed!

One day in the middle of winter, a Hare and a Fox took a walk together. It was during a hard frost. The ground was covered with snow. Not a bit of green grass was to be seen, and there was nothing moving about, not even a mouse or a rabbit.

"This is hungry weather," said the Fox to the Hare. "My limbs ache with cold."

"It is indeed," answered the Hare. "Not a morsel of food to be found anywhere. I could almost eat my own ears if I could only manage to get them into my mouth."

In this hungry mood they trotted along side by side. After some time they saw a peasant girl coming towards them with a large basket in her hand. Out of the basket came a smell which was very pleasant to the Fox and Hare - the refreshing smell of new rolls.

"I'll tell you what we will do," said the Fox. "Lie down full length on the ground and pretend you are dead. When the girl comes up, she will put down her basket to pick you up for the sake of your poor skin, for hareskins make the best gloves. While she is doing this, I will run off with the breadbasket, and we shall have something to comfort us this cold day."

The Hare did just as the Fox bid her. She lay down and pretended to be dead, whilst the Fox hid himself behind a snowdrift. Soon the girl came up, observed the Hare with its legs all stretched out, and put down her basket as the Fox had said she would. She stooped to pick up the Hare. In a moment the Fox jumped out of his hiding place, snatched up the basket, and was off with it like a shot across the fields. The Hare, coming to life again, scampered after her companion. But Sir Fox showed no inclination to stop and share the rolls. He evidently intended to eat them all himself. The Hare did not at all approve. However, she did not utter a word, until they came up to a small pond.

The Hare said to the Fox: "How nice it would be if we could get a dish of fish too! Then we should have fish and white bread, just like the great folks. Suppose you dip your tail in the water, and the fishes, which have not much to bite at just now, will hang on to it. But you must not lose any time about it, or the pond will be frozen."

The Fox thought that some fish would be a great relish with the rolls. He went down to the pond, which was on the point of freezing, and hung his tail in. After a few minutes the tail was fast frozen in, and the poor Fox was a prisoner. Then the Hare took the breadbasket from under the Fox's nose, and ate up the rolls one after the other as coolly as possible, saying to him, "Stop there now until it thaws. You have only to wait till the spring comes. Wait for the thaw."

And then the Hare ran off and left the poor Fox barking after her like an angry dog chained to a post.

## The tale of a mouse

*These children thought it was fun to torture this poor mouse. By tying his tail in this manner, they are destroying the mouse's backbone. A nineteenth-century newspaper printed this picture to remind children of the suffering caused to animals by thoughtless cruelty.*

41

*Susie is crying. She finds it hard to always play by the rules.*

# Strict rules for children

Children of the nineteenth century were brought up strictly by their parents. Often it must have seemed that there was very little they could do right, except to sit quietly. Children with a lot of energy, who made a lot of noise and who ran around, were called "bad children." If someone labeled a child "wicked" or "nasty," there was very little that the child could do to change those labels. Word would get around the community. People would expect that child always to misbehave. In the end, the child would usually do what others expected him or her to do. It was difficult to break the vicious circle. In the following stories and poems, you will meet several children who respond to the people around them in many different ways. *Bully Billy Murphy* performs a heroic deed and manages to change people's opinions of him. *Wicked Willy* behaves badly so that he will be noticed. He ends up without any friends. *Sam Brown* feels sorry for his bad deeds when he realizes how much his sister loves him. *Little Mischief* creates trouble, but is forgiven because he is so young and there is hope for him yet. *Sulky Sally* always frets about what others think of her. She is unhappy because there are too many rules to follow.

Authors tried to scare children into behaving well by writing stories about the dreadful things that happened to children who behaved poorly. In their stories and poems, writers praised the deeds of "good" children. In poems such as *My Loving Nurse* and *Wishes for the Future,* two children are applauded for their kindness and good nature. *Happy Anna* and Martha Finch in *The Magic of Friendship* are held up as examples of loyal and caring children.

The prairie girl of *Predicates and Calves* is punished by her aunt for not showing interest in the things girls are supposed to love doing, such as learning grammar. In those days, people expected girls to act one way, and boys to act another. There were strict differences between the two ways of behaving. Today both boys and girls do the same things.

In *My Dolly* a little girl tells why her dolly is so perfect. The doll always does what she is told and never behaves badly. Maybe the little girl is angry about the fact that she can not be so perfect. In the last line of the poem she admits that the dolly is not as good as a human. Perhaps her mother should appreciate the fact that even if the little girl is not perfect, she at least can offer love.

# Sulky Sally

Sally's sulky, something's wrong,
She is moping all day long.

What's the matter? Why do you pout?
Pray, what is it all about?

During lessons I missed once,
And they called me 'Little Dunce!'

Silly Sally, that's your way
Of existing every day!

Brooding, fretting, all the day,
Always minding what 'they' say.

Foolish Sally, do not cry;
Come, be cheerful – only try!

*Sally sulks about her unhappy day at school. She did not know her lesson.*

# My Dolly

Who lies so calmly in my lap,
And takes, whene'er I please, a nap,
Nor heeds me if I kiss or slap?
              My Dolly.

Who always looks 'as good as gold,'
Nor smiles less if I frown or scold,
And ne'er grows cross, however old?
              My Dolly.

Her bright blue eyes are open wide,
They never had a fault to hide;
No wonder they have never cried, –
              My Dolly.

I hold her gently in my arm,
I fain would shield her from all harm,
But I can't kiss her cold cheeks warm,
              My Dolly.

*A doll has no faults, but can not love.*
*A child has many faults, but can love.*

*Little Mischief, in the picture above, gets his way most of the time. People forgive him easily because he is still small and looks so sweet. As he grows older he will learn that some wrongs just can not be righted.*

# Full of mischief

Along the fields and over the stile
He rushes with little bare feet;
The elm will screen him well for a while,
And the flowers are gay and sweet.

Mother, with half her work undone,
Will seek for him everywhere –
She may stray through the corn in the reddening sun,
She may call, for he does not care.

Today, while mother was yet asleep,
His way to the fold he found,
And then for frolic he sent the sheep
Across the garden ground.

The lettuce was trampled to the earth,
And the rose leaves far were driven;
He was so small, so full of mirth,
This time was he forgiven.

44

Some tears in hasty sorrow fell,
And quiet and good was he;
Then sister Janet heard him spell
In the shade of the alder tree.

The canary's cage in the porch hung low,
And she left him watching by;
When the fields lay hushed in the evening
glow
He let the canary fly!

He hides, but his heart will melt at last,
He longs for his mother's love;
Oh! in her loving arms to be clasped
Ere the stars shine out above!

He must be gentle, meek, and good,
And kind to sister Jane,
For the canary lost in the whispering
wood
Will never come back again!

# Bedtime

The old clock on the mantel
Has chimed the hour of eight;
Papa has issued orders
The children must not wait.

Mamma, in spite of protest,
Enforces the command;
She captures both the rebels,
Holds one in either hand.

These tyrants of the household,
That rule with dreadful power,
Their scepter yield at bedtime;
The clock has chimed the hour.

She leads them through the parlor
And gently up the stairs;
The mystery of undressing
Is followed now by prayers.

When all the rites are over
The last goodnight is said,
Mamma pulls up the cover
And tucks them both in bed.

Brown: *Do those dogs up your way still
continue to howl all night?*
Jones: *No, the dogs have given up in
disgust since our twins arrived on
the scene.* ➤

*Bedtime is a bad time no matter what
century you live in.*

## The howling duo

*Wicked Willie had an upside-down view of life. Instead of wanting to be good, he was always bad. People always expected the worst from him and he lived up to their expectations.*

# Wicked Willie

Willie was a wicked boy,
Snubbed his poor old mother;
Willie was a dreadful boy,
Quarreled with his brother;
Willie was a spiteful boy,
Often pinched his sister;
Once he gave her such a blow,
Raised a great big blister!

Willie was a sulky boy,
Sadly plagued his cousins;
Often broke folks' window panes,
Throwing stones by dozens.
Often worried little girls,
Bullied smaller boys;
Often broke their biggest dolls,
Jumped upon their toys.

If he smelt a smoking tart,
Willie longed to steal it;
If he saw a pulpy peach,
Willie tried to peel it;
Could he reach a new plum cake,
Greedy Willie picked it;
If he spied a pot of jam,
Dirty Willie licked it.

If he saw a poor old dog,
Wicked Willie whacked it;
If it had a spot of white,
Silly Willie blacked it.
If he saw a sleeping cat,
Horrid Willie kicked it;
If he caught a pretty moth,
Cruel Willie pricked it.

If his pony would not trot,
Angry Willie thrashed it;
If he saw a clinging snail,
Thoughtless Willie smashed it;
If he found a sparrow's nest,
Unkind Willie hid it;
All the mischief ever done,
Folks knew Willie did it.

No one liked that horrid boy,
Can you wonder at it?
None who saw his ugly head,
Ever tried to pat it.
No one took him for a ride –
Folks too gladly skipped him;
No one gave him bats or balls,
No one ever "tipped" him.

No one taught him how to skate,
Or to play at cricket;
No one helped him if he stuck
In a prickly thicket.
Oh, no! for the boys all said
Willie loved to tease them,
And that if he had the chance,
Willie would not please them.

And they shunned him, every one,
And they would not know him;
And their games and picture books
They would never show him.
And their tops they would not spin,
If they saw him near them;
And they treated him with scorn,
Till he learned to fear them.

They all left him to himself,
And he was so lonely;
But of course it was his fault,
Willie's own fault only.
If a boy's a wicked boy,
Shy of him folks fight then;
If it makes him dull and sad,
Why it serves him right then!

46

# Sorry Sam

Sam Brown was the strangest of boys;
A ruder you scarcely could see;
His delight was in making a noise,
And trying how rough he could be.
He'd stand by the window and catch a
poor fly,
Then tear off its wings, and just leave
it to die.

His sister, a fair little maid,
With eyes of the tenderest blue,
And clustering curls on her head,
He'd bully and frighten her, too.
He broke her new doll, and picked out
both its eyes,
And laughed when he saw her distress
and surprise.

One day he had gone to the fair,
Resolved on some mischief to do,
When seeing a donkey stand there,
He pinched it and struck at it too.
But the donkey was vicious, and caught
with its teeth,
And shook him till Sam scarce could get
back his breath.

All trembling, and covered with mud,
He crept home in a sorrowful plight,
While all the good folk looking on
Cried out, "Serves the naughty boy right!"
But Anna, his sister, who felt for his
grief,
With tears in her eyes sought to give him
relief.

So gently she bathed his poor head,
And washed all the mud from his hair,
Then seated herself by his bed
To help him his trouble to bear.
"Dear Sam, I will lend you my books if
you choose;"
While Sam, all repenting, could scarcely
refuse.

He grieved o'er the beautiful doll
Which Anna had thought such a prize;
Oh! how could he ever have wished
To poke out its beautiful eyes!
He thought it all over, and made up his
mind
To buy her a new one, the best he could
find.

Then when he grew better he said,
"Dear Anna, I'm glad you forgive;
For never again will I tease
Or vex you as long as I live.
I'm glad I have got such a sister as you,
So kind and forgiving, so tender and true."

*Sam Brown was also called a "bad boy."
However, his sister Anna cured his bad
nature with care and kindness.*

# Happy Anna

She moved about the house like a sunbeam.
I heard her singing as she passed to and
fro, and her mother heard her too, and
she said with a fond smile, "Is it Anna?
She is always the same - always happy."

"I do not know what any of us would do
without her," repeated the eldest daughter,
and the rest echoed her words. Her
youngest brother is of a violent temper,
and is always quarreling with somebody;
but he never quarrels with Anna, because
she will not quarrel with him, but strives
to turn aside his anger by gentle words.
Even her presence has an influence over
him. "A soft answer turneth away wrath,
but harsh words stir up anger."

47

*The little nurse takes a snack up to her sick mother. Children were expected to care for their parents when their parents were ill.*

# My loving nurse

Little fingers ever willing,
Never idle all the day;
Little footsteps softly treading,
Rarely finding time for play;
Little wise head always pondering,
Thinking what can best be done;
What could I e'er do without you
Little Amy, darling one?

Better than all other nurses
You are to me lying here;
All the place seems glad with sunshine
When I hear your footstep near.
Little daughter, He who sent me
Sickness by His own good Will,
Sent thee also in His pity
All my days with joy to fill.

48

*Magic lanterns were old-fashioned slide projectors. The picture was placed into the lantern in front of the light. The image was projected onto a wall or sheet. Magic lanterns delighted children of all ages.*

# The magic of friendship

Martha Finch was a little girl who had lost both of her parents, and was left in the care of an uncle and aunt. They were very poor. Her uncle was an invalid. Her aunt had to work very hard to make a living, taking in washing and doing other odd jobs. Martha, being a very grateful girl, helped her aunt as much as she possibly could. But sometimes in winter she had a very hard time of it, poor little thing! She had to hang out wet clothes on the line in the yard. Now and then she could be seen clapping her poor red hands together to bring into them a little warmth. But she never complained. She fully knew it was a duty she owed her uncle and aunt, who were as kind to her as their means would allow.

One bitter cold day she was busy at the clothesline, when she was called into the house. She found the Reverend Mr. Goodman visiting her uncle. The good clergyman shook her by the hand, and gave her a ticket to go to the church and see the Christmas tree and magic lantern show.

Martha was beside herself with joy. She had never had anything to look forward to before but her work. This opportunity was like a ray of sunshine that had made its way into her otherwise cloudy world. That special evening she went to the church. Her eyes sparkled with delight. They mirrored the flickering glow of the Christmas candles. She had heard of Christmas trees before, but she had never imagined one so beautifully decorated. And the magic lantern simply took her breath away.

After that wonderful evening Martha did her chores with a smile. She had made a new friend, Lucy Lang, at the party. From then on Lucy and Martha went to Sunday school together each week. Martha discovered a joy even greater than that created by the magic lantern. She now had the love and companionship of children her own age.

*Darcy had the slippery reins in his hands, but he was paralyzed with fear.*

# Bully Billy becomes a buddy

Darcy Shipley and his brother, Jesse, sat patiently waiting in their father's carriage. They had stopped in front of the general store. Mr. Shipley was getting some nails. He was building a new chicken coop.

Darcy and Jesse both attended the village school. They had many friends. Billy Murphy, however, was not one of them. No one could trust Billy. He was always making trouble. Jesse warily watched Billy approach them. Darcy looked the other way, hoping Billy would not notice him. But, no such luck!

Billy yelled up at Darcy, "I bet you can't even drive a carriage!"

"I can so!" Darcy replied. "Why, I drove this carriage into town this very day."

"We'll soon see about that!" threatened Billy. Just as he finished uttering his threat, he took an apple from the barrel in front of the store and threw it at the horse's eye.

The horse backed against the carriage, reared up, and started to run. Darcy, having been caught off guard, let out a high-pitched howl. The horse took it as an invitation to go even faster. Off the carriage clattered down Main Street. Every object in its way made the thoroughly frightened horse swerve and speed up.

Darcy and his brother bounced and bawled as they clung, terrified, to the high seat of the carriage. The horse raced past the town limits and stretched his legs even farther as he saw the open road.

His nostrils were wide and his mouth foamed. The carriage swayed like a ship on a stormy sea. Darcy had the slippery reins in his hands, but even so he was paralyzed with fear. His eyes rolled as much as the horse's eyes did. All Jesse could do was hold on for dear life.

Suddenly, from the corner of his eye, Darcy saw Billy galloping beside him on a horse he must have "borrowed." The

carriage horse must have thought he was in a race, for he went even faster. Darcy saw Billy pointing at his hands, which were still frozen on the reins. But Darcy was too frightened to understand what Billy wanted.

Billy inched closer to the head of Darcy's horse. Suddenly, Darcy saw Billy lean down dangerously to grab the reins just where they attached to the bridle. Billy said loudly but calmly, "Whoa, boy, whoa!"

Miraculously, the carriage stopped.

After his brave rescue of Darcy, the whole town cheered Billy. He had become an instant hero. Then Billy did something he had never done before. He apologized to someone. He told Darcy and Jesse that he was sorry for nearly causing a dreadful accident.

Darcy also realized something for the first time. Darcy suddenly understood that Billy had always done terrible things to people to make them notice him. If Billy could be a hero just once, perhaps he would no longer have to be the town bully. Darcy accepted the apology.

After that, Darcy and Billy became good friends. Billy's reputation changed. He became known for his good deeds and thoughtfulness.

## On another note!

"Did he really like my singing?" asked the girl eager to please her new fiancé.
"Oh, yes!" answered her father, "He said it was heavenly."
"Did he really say that?"
"Well, not exactly – but he probably meant that. He said it was unearthly."

*Someone's eight years old today.*

# Wishes for the future

Someone's eight years old today,
  So they say;
Someone who is good as gold,
  I am told;
Someone who has strength of lung,
  Length of tongue,
And the freedom of a bird,
  I have heard.
Someone is a little thing
  Who can sing
With expression - and without,
  There's no doubt.
Someone is a winsome child,
  And not wild,
Like most children; and as shrewd
  As she's good.
Someone's patient, someone's meek -
  Does not shriek
When she cannot have her way.
  Someone's gay,
Kind, obedient, I hear -
  Little dear!
Someone, by her ways and wiles,
  Wins sweet smiles,
Kind words, and of kisses, too,
  Not a few.
Someone's good in every way,
  People say.
May she be in maidenhood
  Just as good;
May she be throughout her life,
  As a wife,
Mother, granny, old and gray,
  What they say
She is now; and find in health
  (Nature's wealth),
Family's love, and friends' regard,
  Rich reward!

# Birthdays

Born on a Monday
       Fair of face
Born on a Tuesday
       Full of grace
Born on a Wednesday
       Merry and glad
Born on a Thursday
       Sour and sad
Born on a Friday
       Godly given
Born on a Saturday
       Work for a living
Born on a Sunday
       Never shall want

*Work for a living.*

*We gathered wildflowers for mother's bouquet, and lovingly wished her a happy birthday.*

# Remembering Mother

A beautiful midsummer morning brought round my mother's birthday. I remember how anxiously we looked forward to the time that we might show our mother, by our little offering and simple words of welcome to the day, how much we loved her.

Early on that morning we rose from our pillow to ramble into the woods, while the dew was yet upon the grass, to pluck the wildflowers for our mother's bouquet. She loved wildflowers, and she taught us to admire the "lilies of the field."

Even now as an adult I feel myself a child again when I recall to mind what trouble my sister and I took to make those flowers a birthday present worthy of our mother's keeping. How timidly, yet how lovingly, we approached her to offer to her the gathered treasures. I feel her kiss upon my cheek. I hear her words of thanks. The look of pleasure on her face appears before me now, in memory. I recall her now as vividly as on the morning she looked so lovingly and tenderly on our childlike offering. Yes, little readers, it is when we grow old that we more fully value a father's love and a mother's tenderness.

*"Nellie was a wild horse. She came to graze in our pasture field. Learning to ride her was quite a challenge!"*

# Hunting for predicates and calves

It must have been in the first spring of our settler life that Auntie took my education in hand. She was determined to lay it on a firm foundation, so she began with grammar. Ye gods! What a thing to offer a wild prairie child of eight. But she kept firmly on and very soon I was completely lost in a thicket of nouns and adjectives, of subjects and predicates. There were articles, adverbs, and pronouns to trip me up at every step.

I stumbled on, not understanding at all what I was doing. Pretty soon disaster followed and then punishment.

Anyway, I hated being a little girl. A boy's work exactly suited me. I could not tell an adverb from an adjective in my grammar puzzles. However, I could quickly find a newborn calf hidden by its mother in the wide-stretching prairie.

## Pluto, Nellie, and I receive our mission

Our cattle used to range at large over the open prairie. When a cow calved she would hide the calf. Then some two days later she would present herself along with the rest of the cows at milking time. Then would come the order for me to find the calf. The plan was as follows: Pluto, my dog, was at once summoned, and came with joyous yelps. Nellie, my horse, was caught and saddled. Nellie lived in the pasture field, so as to be always on hand for emergencies such as this.

When Nellie was wanted, I had only to hold my two well-salted brown paws out to her and call her to me. She was crazy about salt! She would begin by making wide circles around me. By degrees she came nearer and nearer. She would finally come close to lick the salt in my hand. I would then be able to put the reins over her neck and bridle her.

## Fooling mother cow

Nellie, Pluto, and I took the newly calved cow as the center of our circle. We galloped with wild whoops and barks straight away from her towards the north a short distance. We would then stop and look at the cow. If she showed no interest in our noise, we would come slowly back to her and repeat our whooping and hollering in a southerly direction. Again, if that failed, we would direct our course towards the west. The cow would begin to follow when we headed in the direction of the calf's hiding place. She felt she had to protect her newborn from the harm we might bring to it.

In this instance she followed us west. We zigzagged in front of her to the left and to the right. She followed only if our course was right on. If the calf was north-west and we were heading south-west, the cow did not follow. By this trial and error method we were able to pinpoint the exact hiding place of the calf.

*"Sometimes I had to find as many as three calves in a week. I did not mind one bit. The more time I spent hunting calves, the less time I had for battling subjects and predicates."*

## The object of our search

A cow has two bugle calls in her register: one meaning "lie low," which is soft and smooth, and the other meaning "jump and run," which is sharp, quick, and hard. Both are always obeyed by the newborn calf. As soon as we got near the hidden calf the first bugle call in the register sounded continuously. Pluto ranged back and forth through the low cottonwood scrub. I sat motionless on my little saddle waiting for the calf to appear. The second bugle call rang out. With a happy cry, the calf bounded out to join its mother. We returned home in triumph with our captives. Could the finding of a dozen predicates compare in excitement and glory with the finding of a single calf?

55

*Two ways of looking at the world.*

# Blue and yellow

In a pretty house on a hill were two windows. One window was of blue glass, and the other was of yellow glass. Two children entered the place, and looked at the view from the different windows.

"Oh!" cried he who looked through the yellow glass, "What a glorious day is this! How everything is bright with sunshine and white snow!"

"Why, all seems damp and dreary to my eyes," said the other, who was looking through the blue glass. "I'm sure there is sleet falling and frost on every leaf. I see no sunshine at all!"

A cheerful temper is like the yellow glass that makes everything look bright. A peevish temper is like the blue glass, which turns a beautiful day into a miserable day.

# Father's return

Who has a welcome for Father?
For, oh! he has toiled all day,
And now he is glad to come home and rest,
And put all his cares away.

Is tea all ready for Father?
Is the room all tidy and trim?
Does the fire burn bright? Is the hearth
swept clean?
For all must be cosy for him.

Is the pinafore clean for father?
Is the hair brushed smooth and neat?
And are there pleasant words and smiles
In store for him when you meet?

Run, run with a welcome to Father;
Run, bright and tidy and trim:
His turn will come some day to welcome
you,
When you have worked hard for him.

*The children wait for father to return.*

# The butterflies

Flitting o'er a meadow
Went two butterflies,
One of simple yellow,
One of many dyes.

Passing near the other,
Said the bright and gay:
"You look nothing, brother,
In that plain array!"

Scarce had this been uttered,
When a boy came past -
Chased the many-colored,
Till he held him fast.

Still the yellow safely
O'er the meadow sped,
Thanking fate that made him
Without gold or red.

*Being beautiful may be dangerous to
your health.*

# Story starters

By now you have read many poems and stories written for and about the settlers. It is time for you to try your hand at writing. We have started some poems and stories for you. Your job is to complete them. So sharpen your quills, and dip them into the inkwells. Write away!

**1** Ten pussycats took the stagecoach one day,
To visit their cousins who lived far away.
It was just before Christmas, they had presents in store,
For each of their cousins they had surprises galore!
In a hurry they urged the hound to run,
When the cats in the coach heard the shot of a gun ....

**2** These children were lost and found. The tale ends with the following line: "Bess gave a cry of joy, and ran to wake the children." Can you think of a beginning ◄ and a middle for the story?

**3** There was an old sleigh on top of a hill, And ten daring boys who wanted a thrill. The moon was up over the sleepy town, When the boys climbed in and the sleigh went down! ....

**4** Violet and Rose were collecting seashells by the shore. "Be home before the tide comes in," their mother had warned them. But there they were, caught on the rocks. The path home was cut off by the rising water ....

**5** The Middleton children lived on the prairies. They had lost their mother and father in a prairie storm. They were taken in by the Brown family, their nearest neighbors. Mr. and Mrs. Brown were not very kind to the children. They made them work in the fields from morning to night.

One night the children crept from their beds to write a letter to their aunt who ◄ lived in the east ....

## Popcorn

CHARACTERS

Mrs. Van Elspeth, *a poor woman*

Teddy Van Elspeth, *her son, a cripple*

Alice Franklyn, *a young lady*

Herbert Franklyn, *Alice's brother*

Tom Leslie, *Alice's cousin*

Miss Murray, *a governess, and Alice's friend*

The scene must shift from Mrs. Van Elspeth's house, which must be poor and very barely furnished, to Miss Franklyn's parlor, prettily and richly adorned. A screen, two or three rugs, a lamp, and some pictures on the wall will make the rooms full or bare, as a scene change is needed. A stove for the making of popcorn must be used in Mrs. Van Elspeth's apartment. Mrs. Van Elspeth wears a calico gown, with a white kerchief crossed over her shoulders. She should have on a nurse's cap and a full white apron. Miss Franklyn and Miss Murray may appear in pretty house dresses. Any ordinary boy's costume will do for the young gentlemen.

## ACT I

Mrs. Van Elspeth's *kitchen. She is busy popping corn, which* Teddy *salts and puts into paper bags.*


TEDDY:

I'm afraid, mammy dear,
That our Thanksgiving dinner
Will lack of good cheer,
And leave us both thinner.
I've done my best, mother,
But popcorn is down,
And few people buy it
In this selfish town.
I'd try something else,
But one cannot do much
Who hobbles about
As I do on a crutch.
Please, mammy, consent,
Let me jump on the trains,
And I'll sell my popcorn
With a good deal less pains.
Folks are tired of sitting
Like sheep behind bars;
They will buy from me
If I'm seen on the cars.

MRS. VAN ELSPETH:

My darling son, I've done my best,
I've scoured and scrubbed like one
possessed;
I've washed, I've ironed, and I've
swept,
I've mended clothes when others slept;
I've gone out nursing, taken orders
For magazines, and I've kept boarders;
Sold eggs at market, peddled candy,
Done all things honest that came handy;
And here, as I am growing thinner,
I cannot earn a common dinner;
Say nothing of the sumptuous living
That people reckon is Thanksgiving.

TEDDY:

Oh! see that corn;
It feathers white
Like snowflakes on
A wintry night.

MRS. VAN ELSPETH:

'Tis pretty, Teddy boy, I own;
But what's the use, there'll no one buy
The dainty stuff; they only laugh
At sounding of your popcorn cry.

TEDDY, *jumping up and waving his crutch, cries shrilly:*

Pop-cor-r-r-n!
Fresh pop-cor-r-r-n!
Snowy white and
S-a-a-a-lted!

That'll get them, mammy dear,
Nicest corn I've sold all year.

MRS. VAN ELSPETH, *putting aside the corn-popper, and sighing wearily:*

You may try your luck on the four
fifteen,
I *may* be wrong, but I do not know;
If you sell every bag, you will have
two dollars;
It's too much to hope for, Ted, but go.

Teddy, *basket on arm, stumps sturdily away on his crutch. A whistle sounds in the distance. He hurries along hoping to catch the train, when he stumbles and falls heavily, losing his basket, out of which the bags of popcorn roll in every direction.* Miss Murray *appears, coming from behind a screen, which is supposed to be the front door of the* Franklyn's *cottage.*


MISS MURRAY:

Oh, *poor* little boy, what a pity is this!
You are lame too, and hurt very much,
I'm afraid;
And here's your popcorn, 'tis all scat-
tered, forlorn,
The very best popcorn that ever was
made.
Come, I'll help pick it up. You were
going to sell it?
Now *we* want popcorn to string up in
the halls,
We've a festival night planned, we'll
send you to tell it,
And paste up the news on the citizens'
walls.
Don't be worried, poor fellow, 'tis almost
Thanksgiving,
The jolliest time, full of peace and good
living.

TEDDY:

Thank you, lady
I must hurry,
Mother'll have
No end of worry

I *must* sell these popcorn balls;
We are just as poor as mice,
Won't *you* buy some?
They are salted, and are very, very
nice.

MISS MURRAY:

The train has gone, but come with me,
And see my friends - here's Herbert now!

HERBERT:

Hallo! Ted!
Are you in business?

TEDDY:

Trying it, with poor success.

HERBERT:

Tom! Tom! Come here, I say,
Here's a fellow, you understand,
Who will give us a chance in the good
old way,
That Alice says, is to lend a hand!


ACT II

Miss Franklyn, *sitting in a low chair, with
a gray pussycat on her lap. Bits of silk
and worsted scattered about her.* Miss
Murray, *at the piano, playing and singing
softly to the tune of "Annie Laurie."*

Thanksgiving snow is whiter
Than any snow that falls,
Thanksgiving suns are brighter
Then lamps in palace halls.

Tom, *bouncing in, boy fashion, and
upsetting a footstool, frightening the
cat, and causing* Miss Murray *to frown
and uplift her hand in warning.*

TOM:

I say, Alice, and Miss Murray,
Hustle round, my dears, and hurry,
Ted, the popcorn boy, has fainted,
Herbert says, be quick, you're wanted!

ALICE:

Fainted! Lay him flat,
And fan him.
Who is Ted, the popcorn boy?

MISS MURRAY:

Such a manly little fellow!

HERBERT:

Fellow with a crutch; his mother
Takes in sewing down the street.

TOM:

I don't think that Ted Van Elspeth
Ever gets enough to eat!

ALICE:

Ted Van Elspeth?
Josephine, don't you think we knew her
In the old days when we two,
Hand in hand, 'neath skies so blue,
Went for berries and for nuts?
She made splendid lemonade,
And when dear papa was injured,
She his best of nurses made.
She nursed me that dreadful summer
When I had a fever here.
Ted Van Elspeth, we will aid you,
You have found the right place, dear.

TOM:

This is really very jolly,
Turnabout is fairest play;
We will take him to his mother
In the most luxurious way;
In a carriage, if he pleases.

*Enter* Mrs. Van Elspeth.
MRS. VAN ELSPETH:

Where's my Ted,
With the golden head,
And the cheeks as red as roses?
Where's my Ted?
Somebody said
He wasn't seen on the train!

TOM:

Mrs. Van Elspeth, here is Ted,
He has sold his popcorn out.
Why do you cry? He's here close by,
Don't be making a fuss about
His looking white, it is only pleasure,
His wares have brought him such rare
good measure.

ALICE:

My dear old nurse!
Pray take this purse!
You'll find sufficient in it
To make Thanksgiving all the year,
Thanksgiving every minute.

*All join hands, dance around the stage,
and the curtain drops.*

# Glossary

account  *a record of events; description*
adjective  *a "describing" word, e.g., "pretty"*
adjoining  *next to each other*
adverb  *a word used to describe how something is done, e.g., "quickly"*
article  *a word such as "a" or "an" or "the" which is put before a noun*
awry  *on the side*
bawl  *to cry out noisily*
bemire  *to dirty with mud*
blizzard  *a severe snowstorm*
boarder  *someone who lives in a house, receiving meals and a bed in return for money*
breeches  *knee-length trousers*
calve  *to give birth to a calf*
chime  *the sound made by a bell*
comical  *funny*
conservation  *the prevention of waste, loss or decay*
cut a caper  *to play*
dabble  *to play*
delirious  *raving and restless due to a fever*
diphtheria  *a disease which produces fever and great weakness*
drove (of cattle)  *a group of animals herded or driven*
ere  *before*
err  *to make a mistake*
fain  *gladly*
floe  *a large piece of floating ice*
foe  *enemy*
gambol  *to leap about happily*
headway  *progress; forward motion*
hearth  *a stone space in front of a fireplace*
hide  *the skin of an animal*
indignation  *anger*
invalid  *an unwell or bedridden person*
Jack Frost  *the name given to frost or winter weather*
lay  *a song*
limb  *an arm or a leg*
loft  *a floored space directly under a roof*
mastiff  *a hunting dog*
means  *money, property, or other resources*
menace  *to scare someone; a troublesome person or pest*
mien  *manner, expression, or outward appearance*
moral  *the lesson about life contained in a poem or story*
morsel  *a small bit of food*
mute  *silent*
newt  *a lizard*
nigh  *near*

noun  *a word used as the name of a person, a place, or a thing, e.g., "fish," "tent"*
palings  *the upright stakes which form a fence*
peddle  *to travel about selling something in small quantities*
peevish  *fretful, complaining, irritated*
pinafore  *a sleeveless apronlike garment, worn to protect a child's dress*
pollen  *a fine, yellowish, powderlike substance, part of a flower*
pound  *a place where lost animals are kept*
precipice  *the edge of a steep cliff*
predicate  *the part of a sentence which contains the verb, and often the object*
press coverage  *the articles and stories in newspapers, magazines, etc., concerning an event or person*
pronoun  *a word used instead of a noun, e.g., "she", "he", "we", "they", "it"*
quartet  *a group consisting of four things of the same kind*
ramble  *to wander about*
register  *the sounds a voice or instrument can make*
relish  *something eaten with food to give it more flavor*
reputation  *the way a person is thought of by other people*
rite  *an important ceremony*
rivalry  *competition*
scepter  *a stick which shows that the person carrying it has power*
shrewd  *wise; clever*
sleet  *a mixture of snow and rain*
stile  *steps on each side of a fence which help a person get over the fence*
sty  *the place where pigs are kept*
subject  *the main idea in a sentence*
succumb  *to give in to something; to die*
sumptuous  *luxurious; gorgeous*
thicket  *a thick growth of small bushes*
trundle bed  *a low bed which can be stored under another bed*
vagrant  *wandering about without a home*
vapors  *fog*
verdict  *a decision*
vex  *to make someone angry*
visibility  *the ability to see a distant object clearly*
wail  *to cry out in sorrow*
warble  *to sing with trills or vibrations*
wares  *products or goods which are sold*
wiles  *tricks*
winsome  *attractive; pretty*
zeal  *enthusiasm*

# Index

# Acknowledgements

*Library of Congress, Dover Archives, Century Village, Lang, Metropolitan Toronto Library, Harper's Weekly, Canadian Illustrated News, Frank Leslie's Illustrated Magazine, The Osborne Collection of Early Children's Books, Toronto Public Library, The Buffalo and Erie County Public Library Rare Book Department, Chatterbox, Little Wide Awake, Harper's Round Table Magazine, John P. Robarts Research Library, Thomas Fisher Rare Book Library, U of T, William Blackwood and Sons.*  456789 BP Printed in Canada 0987